Saturday at the Gym

by

Janice Lynch Schuster

Janice Lynch Schuster

For Eileen at the
launch of our friendship!
3/23/13

Published by Three Acre Wood Press

421 Granville Road
Riva, MD 21140

Copyright 2011 by Janice Lynch Schuster

ISBN: 978-0-615-45285-2

"Conor Leaves for Europe," "Driving in the Dark," "Holding Dinner," and "Rain, Not Poetry," first appeared in *The Broadkill Review.*

"My Father Breathes" first appeared in *Poet Lore.*

For Erik

Rain, Not Poetry

I was hoping for a poem but instead there came the rain
Gushing over the leaf-laden gutters,
Knocking heads off the hibiscus
And soaking three beach towels left to dry
Overnight on the hot deck.
I was hoping for a poem but instead there came the rain
The noisy fall of it half the night
Till my dreams all turned to water.
I was hoping for a poem that might explain
My life to me, my children's, and a week
Of uncertain loves to which they have grown attached,
From which I wish to shake them,
Much as I wish to shake this rain from my umbrella
And get on with a sunnier day of living.
I was hoping for a poem but instead there came the rain
Interpreting nothing yet touching everything
Even the small blossoms of weeds hidden in the deep woods.

Holding Dinner

Dinner is ready but you are not
Here, traffic or some distraction
Diverts you from home. You never call.
Happy to eat alone, you do not notice
Or care that I have made this dish
For you—peeled grapes, sautéed garlic
Wept over onions and sliced
My own hand, not the chicken breast.
Who am I to you, woman in the house
Where dinner waits? As it is, you are simply
Late and I am tired, standing while I wait
For the sound of your footstep
In the hall, the rattling plate as you reheat
What hours ago was warm.

Driving in the Dark

The controls and pedals stymie her,
So much to think about, backing up
Our tree-lined driveway, a collision course
For the most experienced driver.
She is sixteen and her moves are unsteady,
Tentative here in the dark, unsure.
Like learning to walk, she thinks herself safe
In my presence. We are practicing
Nighttime driving, watching for deer
And oncoming lights, maneuvers
And habits that will last a lifetime.
She sets the mirrors but forgets the headlights.
I sit silent, waiting for her to notice.
The driveway is even dimmer—the red
Taillights illuminate the trees behind us
As we reverse out of darkness
And I wonder what she sees
As I watch the black night
Embrace us like a leather glove,
Tight and seamless.

It is so dark, Mommy, she says,
And just this once, my answer
Is easy and correct, I can direct
Her safely again to the next step
As she illuminates a path
That both of us must follow.

Vintage

He mounts her like a long-time lover.
Familiar, comfortable,
He knows how to make her purr.
They have aged together.
He is patient,
Days when she comes apart,
Nights he spends machining pieces
Making her whole again.
In his silver Kevlar jacket
Sun glints off his back.
He might be 20 when he does 90
And the open road pours out before them
An elixir against the accumulated years
The things that take him from this world.

Aly Dreams of the SATs

She dreams she scores 3,000
On her SATs and the numbers
Transfigure her life. What is the property
Where all things are less and more,
Approaching infinity, and zero,
The less and greater than's compiling
A score no one understands?
Here's the dream: You exceed your worries.
You are more than you are less.
You are everything a number cannot contain.
You are most wondrous, a combination
Of cells and heart, something incalculable,
More than anything we could have compiled.
You are the genius
Of your own life, genesis and generator—
Everything lies before you.
No matter what dreams might come,
You are a whole number,
A calculation, an imaginary world
Of being, my true love, my girl, 3,000
More than 3,000, your own perfect score.

Conor Leaves for Europe

And I am talking about shoes:
What he needs to hike and tour.
He is keen on something dapper,
My bespoke man-child eyes
Boots made of wing-tips, thin soled,
Italian, expensive and sharp.
I suggest something sturdier,
More grounded—bulky, but light.

In a trunk of memories, I have his first pair
Of toddler shoes, from the days his feet
rarely touched the ground.
He raced upstairs and, afraid he would tumble,
I lured him back to me with a lollipop,
My fear invisible to him behind the treat.
I attached bells to the shoes.
Our house rang with exploration.

Conor leaves for Europe.
There will be no more bells,
Though I listen for his progress.
Whether the boots are stylish or stodgy
They will take him away from me.

Wasn't that my job, to set him free,
Wild with his curiosity and longing,
The whole world a flight of stairs,
Me at the bottom, waving him on?

My Father Breathes

When he taught us to swim
Breathing was the hardest part:
How to turn your head
Just so into a pillow of suffocating
Water and suck air from clouds
While keeping the complicated
Body afloat.

I think of those lessons
These days when cancer steals his breath
Frightens him into spasms of gasping
At air so ordinary and vital
We simply assume it's ours.

I offer instructions
For this most basic activity:
Breathe
In deeply through the nose
Gently out through pursed lips
Tongue rolled on the roof of the mouth.

I stand beside him whispering
"Breathe" like a prayer
While he clutches something in
And then
At least for now
Surfaces again.

A Prayer for Meredith

Every day something wonderful is on the verge of happening,
If only you know to concentrate—you feel
The morning sun burning away the clouds
To a God-sky of shimmer and light.
You see the yellow-footed bee dancing through the flowers,
And the red-lush tomato dangling from its vine;
You find a bluejay feather, tropical and wild,
In the brown summer grass, you hear
The nesting woodpecker in the siding of the house.
A translucent snakeskin, lacelike, flies from the dogwood
And the green trees scribble an outline across the horizon.
It is all waiting for you:
Amen to the color of wind.
Hallelujah to the cells of the heart.
Blessings to the sound of your own life.
Rejoice, rejoice, rejoice.

Professional Walker

Before we set out for a walk
on the beach my father cautions
that he is not, like me,
A "professional" walker,
four and a half marathons
Under my belt (or soles),
Hundreds of thousands of steps
From which I learned only this:
I endure.
                I have tattooed the emblem
Of these walks on my ankle—
Two stylized women, arms draped
Around each others' shoulders
Intent on one step.
The walk is all charity
But the stride is all mine.
Two daughters, two sisters,
All the women I love, walking.
        The tattoo artist cuts me a discount,
His mother had breast cancer
And my pink tattoo reminds him
That we are all survivors
Even when we aren't.

Walking on the beach with my father
Nine months into his cancer-free life
We are all survivors here.
His amateur steps
Are a gift this August when the waves
Run rip currents and the water is icy cold,
When the sun blasts down
And we falter a little in the deep, jagged shells.
When we dig holes on the beach
And watch the children body surf.
Our steps leave parallel prints
On the sand, until the waves
Fill them, then retreat.

Drive Safely

Aly mocks my daily admonition
To drive safely, as if she might forget
What she has so recently learned:
To stop and go, to yield and signal.
She does not know how a flash
Of distraction can ignite catastrophe,
How easy it would be
For this machine that she loves
To be an engine of destruction.
All that is not on her mind,
Though it is often on mine,
The incessant worrying voice of motherhood.

Drive safely is my incantation,
A blessing for the words I cannot pronounce—
God bless you, my grandmother used to say
Whenever I left her for a while. I have none
Of that faith to go on. I'm left wishing
For guardian angels, shorthand of a prayer.

Empty Nest

All the years I prayed for quiet
Have come to this
A still house where no one needs
Anything from me. I am free
Except for memory, pulling
With its bright light in the corners,
All the moments we did
And did not deserve.

Those years of counting heads—
five of them lined up on the shore
while we tried to cover them with more
sunblock and life vests, protection, while they screeched
to reach the waves and I tired
with the commotion of their needs,
longed for a bed where I could sleep
alone, no children on the floor
or at the door, no one hungry
or sad, excited or needy,
nights when I worried where they were,
the after-midnight footfalls of their sneaking
home, the stolen cars returned
and everyone safe and loved.

All gone. I am free
to do as I please and here I sit
wondering what I was praying for
those years when sweet heads
nestled to my breast and breathed
the comfort of my presence,
and I, theirs. Now I cradle
empty space, the past, things opening
on the quiet, all that has gone,
the nothings of the space we leave behind.

For Sayed

January 30, 2011

When I stumbled on 18th Street
Sayed lifted me to my feet. We laughed.
What friends do for each other—
The dusting off, the standing upright.
We shared our trivial lives—teenagers driving,
University admissions, vagaries of long marriage,
Our improbable friendship, that we had met
At all, bellydancing on a Tunisian dance floor.
With revolution in the region,
Police bearing down on crowds,
I wonder where Sayed is,
Blocked from the rest of us.
I like to imagine that he is dancing, still,
That we are holding each other up,
That the world spins, and we stand.

Osage-Orange

The osage-orange wood arrives express,
six-feet delivered UPS, in a box
quickly hidden in the garage, where tools
and treasures disappear, only to resurface
when he manufactures something of nothing.
A handyman, he is never still.
His restless hands now focus on a bow.
He watches "Robin Hood" and sands
the osage-orange, leaving a spray-paint yellow dust
on everything he touches. His clothes
shine with it. He tells me he can see the bow
in the wood, suggests I spot it, too—
my imagination does not stretch that far—
but he planes and tillers until something emerges,
curved, almost propeller-like, smooth
the age rings making a grain against the wood.
He embraces it when he takes aim
at a little box set up in the woods
and shoots. The eternal boy in him
would jump with excitement, but the man
stays grounded. The arrow flies true.
The shavings dust his feet.

Sleepless, Depression

Sleepless nights. My inadequacies accumulate
Like snow, covering everything, leaving nothing
But shapes of what things are.
Depression does it to me, heavy,
Cold, relentless, a storm in which my failures
Line up for review. Where to start
Blaming myself? That unforgiving voice
Is there, full-throated and ready
To condemn. All the things I did not know
To do—or knew and did anyway—
The years lost to crazy combinations
Of depression and stress, the mind,
My own, but on a path I did not devise.
All the regrets drifting to the door of memory.
If I let them in, they will overwhelm
The small house I have constructed,
What warmth I have harbored there.
These sleepless nights, my shortcomings weigh
The balance of my life. Try though I might
To brush them aside, they come in
Through the cracks.

Boxing in Bifocals

I wear them so I can read
The fine print
On my opponent's gloves

Like a Girl

My trainer admires
My form—perfect, strong—
I did not know it was mine

Swinging

Jab cross uppercut jab
Cadence of punches stopping
Heavy bag swinging

Teaching the Girls

After dinner the girls shadow box
In the kitchen. There is small space
For their joy, their blonde energy
As they bob and weave near the counter.

I warn them about the burners,
coffee pot and knives.
Metaphors fly; they are merry and warm,
I am their crazy coach, reciting
Combinations as what's left of dinner burns.

Chin down, guard up!
Light on your feet,
Snap that punch!

I've been training them for years
For the punches life will land,
The world beautiful and brutal,
Everyday and extraordinary.

I want them ready to slip
Through it as we do this night,
So wired by their own lives,
Nothing crowding them in a corner
The whole arena of my love
Resounding in their laughter.

Engage the Hips

So many years spent regretting them:
Too broad, flabby, wide
For jeans, precursors to thighs.
I could never love
My pear-shaped form.

Now Ron wants them engaged:
They are the center
Of attention. Without their power
My punches go nowhere.
"Work your booty!"
He admonishes and for once
I think they might be worth
Their weight in gold.
"Engage the hips!" he shouts.
Because I can go nowhere
Without them, I listen.

Boxing Lesson

I was not built for this.
These hips bear weight
Spin men and dreams
Not pivots and punches.
Still, I try to defy biology.
Work to train the body
For what it might accomplish,
Something firm,
Unyielding, grounded and on guard.
All the words flesh does not construct
The mind longs to hear.

Boxing Team: Because My Mother Asked

Here is the poetry in this, fists
Jab cross jab cross

Courtney jumps rope. The team
Echoes her footfalls.

Jumping jack cross.
Jumping jack cross.

Her long legs sketch a pattern
In the air. The black rope
Skitters like a snake in the grass,
Here and gone before you
Register its presence.

Jab cross jab cross.

Josh kicks. His dreadlocks swing
In the air, his silhouette
Aligned like an 'I', legs
Twisting like a whirl-i-gig.

Head body head body.

Matt says more violent moves
Will make me faster. But I am slow
Trying to go low and slip
Out of harm's way. *Guard up!*

Jab cross jab cross

The twelve of us dancing
To Ron's i-pod. He leads. We follow,
Synchronized and tired.
Our ropes spin.

Jab cross jab cross

If I ever float like a butterfly
Unwrap my hands
And watch me soar.

Head body head body
Jab jab jab

Wraps

Once we wore them in the evening to guard
Our shoulders against the cold. Now I wind
Them around my outstretched hands.
Fingers spread, I twist the fabric
Into a complex pattern of figure eights
And turns. Knuckles and thumbs wrapped,
Wrists stiff and unyielding, protected
From boxer's fracture.
I leave wedding band on, gold
Flashing beneath the black webbing
Stretched taut around my fists.
I slip on the white gloves
And pound a heavy bag, trying
To keep it still as I slam it
For all I'm worth.
Wraps loosen, the way I once shrugged
Off a black velvet number to display
My glamour muscles.
Nothing glamorous now.
I pull the ends tighter,
Put my guard up in a mask
That reveals nothing but the hands
Wrapped and ready.

Inscriptions

The boxer inscribes his gloves
With a to-do list of furies.
Black ink on yellow leather,
Near the laces pulled so tight
The wrists cannot bend.
 His trainer has made the delicate
Twists of wrapping his hands,
The intimate gestures
Of dressing. He has whispered
Final combinations, as if the boxer
Could forget the hours

Of muscle memory, shadowboxing
And conditioning drills
Breathless minutes
When he could hardly lift
His hands and eyes.
His body fires
With singular knowledge:
Hit, or be hit.

He will not be able
To read the words
With his guard up,
Gloves to his nose.
But he will remember
Them in the final round
When he embraces

His opponent—not like lovers,
But two angry, tired men
Feeling for each other's weakest
Point, vulnerabilities and tender
Places, maneuvering for a final
Blow, whispering secret
Aggressions, waiting
For the other to fall.

Running in the Rain

The mind objects and the knee
The brain insists the feet quit
But they—truly—plod on, one
After another, slogging through puddles,
Intent on this single mile,
Not the brain's singular denial
That I give up the race. My pace
Is slow and steady and will win
No ribbons or personal bests.
Only this, the challenge of the thing,
The way of proving myself wrong
Again, persevering and pounding
Down the road.

You Remember Everything

You remember everything about me.
I remember you, too, how your hands caressed
My body, as if I were gold and you its alchemist.

This fall, the trees riot green, the woods tipped yellow.
Dogwoods rouged in pink, salvia gone all lavender,
The maple gone crimson. It is August

Until you wake up and it's October and life parades
Past in color and you wonder what to wear.
Nothing does justice to the weather or the air.

What you remember changes. I remember this:
You were gone in an instant. Winter just come.
The cold months of your absence became years.

What has become of the hands
I remember so well? That boy you were, almost a man
Who loved me as if nothing could change

This fact of life: I was yours and you mine.
Still are. When I hear your voice I remember
What it means to be loved, to be changed utterly

Like a tree changed by sun, water and time.
Of course I remember everything about you.
You were everything—and then some—to me.

Scratching the Wedding Plans

We elope and have a secret ceremony in Vegas
And the slot machines come up bells,
Golden rings and pierced hearts.
Sirens play the wedding march
And cigarette girls dispense matchbooks
With our names engraved in red.
On the white towering cake a plastic bride
And groom exchange the ace of hearts
And your hand slips down my garter
While the blackjack dealer goes out.
We say, "I do," to everything; neon signs blink
Best wishes and the baccarat tables
Are cleared for a dance floor. Our first
Dance is something worth whistling
And my red dress glows in the dark
Against the folds of your silk suit.
We each take half the guest list
And play numbers based on names.
We are winning at something
And call it love. We are holding hands
And the future reels out like an endless
Classic movie. You are Tracy to my Hepburn
And in the black-and-white air, I see everything.
My eyes hold yours, even when other lights
Come up, even when the sun rises, even here
In the desert, where you can hardly separate
Thirst from desire.

Dancing with Marcian

Twenty years on, I dream we are dancing in the quad,
The air just cooled, our love, just fired.
We are light and inconsequential as the leaves
Lifting under our feet. In the dark, I can barely
See you, but feel your eyes, traveling my body,
Undressing me as if you were the wind
And I, a tree, stripped of leaves, bare,
Waiting in the still air for change to come along.

The alarm sounds
The music stops
For a second only
Your hand is on my cheek
And I am wholly yours again,
Space and time meaning nothing
To those who love.

Coming, Going, for Ian

Soon enough, you will travel
From my arms to your own feet,
From the days I plan for you
To maps of your own design.

Soon enough, you will go
From sleeping at my breast
To sleeping at those of women you will love,
Who might love you as I do.

And before I am ready
You will go from being my child
To fathering your own.

Because all of this takes forever
And is over in no time,
Because mothering is more weaning
Than staying, because you are

My beautiful boy, I want these days
Never to end, and want you to grow
Into the man who tells me why.

From Across America, My Lover Speaks of Rain

And I want to be the rain falling around him,
Trickling through his hair, into his eyes,
Across his lips, over his back, mapping
A terrain of channels, a territory of lakes
And inlets, a bayful of soothing…

He speaks of rain and I want to be
The word on his lips,
The roll of an 'r'
The smile of the long 'a'
The thrusting tongue and teeth of 'n'.

He says, "It is raining," and I want
To be the coat he dons, the hat,
To be draped across his shoulders,
To hold him until our arms replicate
Circles of rain on grass.

He says rain and I want to be the home
He enters, the woman who kisses
His face wetter, or guides his watery
Hand across her breast and says, "Love,"
Because the rainbow forms, just then,
For them.

Metaphysics for a Four-year Old

The Sunday school teacher promises
To leave evil out of things,
But my son insists on knowing:

Who was the devil's mother?

If his guardian angel sleeps
At his side, how do nightmares
Squeeze in around him?

If Jesus takes the dead,
Why pray for them?
If Jesus comes to earth,
What does he drive, and how?
How do you talk to Jesus?
And if he can talk,
Why not write, and if He writes,
Why not send a letter to the dead
Whose angelic faces
Are lonely?

For Erik

So we ran through the fire
Because crawling was an easy escape.
We pushed damp rags
To our mouths and pulled
Children from burning rooms.
It was only our lives
Flaming. Time grafted
Over years of marriage and desire
Until it was loss upon loss upon loss.

And now the cool blue easy
Touch of your hands
Springs from the same source
As do we: human hands are starfish
Trained for dirt,
Elements are separated
By atomic structure
And you and I differ
By a chromosome. In the strength
Of your arms, and the power
Of my own, these differences
Are nothing. I swim

Where once I could not breathe
And laugh where anger
Locked me to loss

And nothing could extinguish
The life of your shadowed face
In the raft of this sleepy bed
And your dreaming hands
Like compresses on wounds
I no longer feel

Family Bed

Between my snoring husband and the restless
Dream hands of our son,
I lie awake, counting anything that moves:
Shadows laced through venetian blinds,
Neighbors opening and closing doors,
Sirens terrorizing the night,
Kicks and somersaults of the unborn child
Who lies awake with me, ghost
In this family bed.

Five kicks an hour are how I count her life,
Securing it against all catastrophes
Of genetics and old indiscretions,
The uterus, the undistinguished flesh
Works a miracle from my body to hers.

My son shouts at me in his sleep,
Reliving the day's unsettled moments:
Spilled milk, unsavory green beans,
Shoes I would not let him wear,
Blanket draped around his feet.
I murmur but he does not hear,
Calms only when his head settles
Against my comfortable night shirt.

His father stirs and mumbles.
I wait for that day when out of his incoherent
Sleep-talk I salvage another woman's name.
Until now, all things rise on faith and hope:
He and I, the children we do not avoid creating,
As if we were Zeus and Hera
Or Joseph and Mary, as if our small lives
Were something far grander,
A mythology of our own in this family bed:

Sleeping and counting
Sleeping and colliding
Sleeping past dawn until
Unmistakable daylight etches
Itself on our faces.

Birds

Pretty birds perish against their reflections
In the only clean window of our house.

You hurl their carcasses into the woods,
Noting once the yellow feathers, but mostly
Aiming for far-away places.

When the survivors return
To the feeders and baths,
I exclaim, "Look at the cardinals!"
Their orange and black faces
Cartoons of birds.

I want to share wonder
But you turn your head
Tell me you've seen birds
Before.

The Scientist Confronts Death

Here is what dies—
Synapses, receptors, dendrites,
Mitochondria, chromosomes,
All the fantastic beauty
The unaided eye never sees.

And these too—organs
Heart and lung, kidney and bladder,
Orbiting the brain
The gravity of life.

And this: coreopsis and heather
Rhododendron and lily
Bleeding heart and cypress
And the human garden
Of the heart.

But never this: the soul
Thriving by its own measure,
Not the world's.

Three-Acre Wood

This is the place to age
Our love, so many corners
For what belongs, enough
Space to fill a life.

These woods will give our days
The shape of trees
And heaven, a horizon
Toward which we will walk

Twining with the underbrush.
We might stop to name
A thousand trees—
Your Adam to my Eve.

Though my temptations all are good,
And the knowledge is simple, love.

What It Takes

What it takes are the fireflies
Arrayed against the twilight
Or jeweled across children
Who can never trap enough.

What it takes is a footstep
On my front porch at dawn
And I hear my grandmother
Coming again for coffee.

And toast, if I'll get it,
And juice, and she comes back
To my waiting heart, as if
She'd never gone,
And I'd never known
This expansive lonely life
Without her, as if we'd never parted
And never would again.

For Conor

Between Kosovo and Colorado
A dark corona takes the landscape
Until every living thing is surrounded.
Evil is as real as the bullet
In a child's gun—fast and deadly.
When he pulls the trigger
The innocent lose everything,
Even the ones not in the room
Or country, even the homeless
Who sleep on dirt in the mountains,
Even the free under the stars,
Even America, which looks like Disneyland,
Even when it's dying.

My little boy asks why bad things
Happen in the West.
I map the terrain of his face
With my eyes, and explain
That we are all West of somewhere,
Though he is safe here.

Saturday at the Gym

Ron's diamond studs glitter as he calls
Commands for me to punch him.
My hands are wrapped and gloved.
"Jab-cross-jab-cross," he says,
Holding up a black mitt
For me to hit, warning me
To guard my face. We are so close
In this connection, bodies pulled
Together and apart. There is an art
To it, though mine is hardly that
As I pound and pound, working
To stay upright and not complain.

He pushes me a few times
So I can feel how it feels.
He does not know that I take
Every punch already,
In my bones and sinews,
Fighting as I am the blinding light
Of my own middle age, my mortality
Roaring out of nowhere, time
After me and gaining
Every minute. I pivot
And throw a hook.
He calls me baby.
In that moment
I'm as young as I'll ever be.

7708729R0

Made in the USA
Charleston, SC
02 April 2011